The Flowering

Paige Stirling Fox

Illustrated by Lena Ralston

Copyright © 2012 Paige Stirling Fox

Illustrations
Lena Ralston

Editor
Sherry Hinman

Promotion and Publicity
Dana Jackson

All rights reserved. No part of this book may be used or reproduced by any means, graphic, electronic, or mechanical, including photocopying, recording, taping or by any information storage retrieval system without the written permission of the publisher except in the case of brief quotations embodied in critical articles and reviews.

ISBN: 978-1-4525-5011-4 (sc)

Library of Congress Control Number: 2012906367

Balboa Press books may be ordered through booksellers or by contacting:

Balboa Press
A Division of Hay House
1663 Liberty Drive
Bloomington, IN 47403
www.balboapress.com
1-(877) 407-4847

Because of the dynamic nature of the Internet, any web addresses or links contained in this book may have changed since publication and may no longer be valid. The views expressed in this work are solely those of the author and do not necessarily reflect the views of the publisher, and the publisher hereby disclaims any responsibility for them.

Any people depicted in stock imagery provided by Thinkstock are models, and such images are being used for illustrative purposes only. Certain stock imagery © Thinkstock.

Printed in the United States of America

Balboa Press rev. date: 4/23/2012

Words of Praise

"The Flowering House *will move your heart and inspire you to journey toward a life of authenticity, truth and purpose. Paige Stirling Fox not only tells a great story, but lives it.*"
Tommy Spaulding, *New York Times* bestselling author of *It's Not Just Who You Know*

"The Flowering House *is a beautiful book of self-discovery that provides practical tools for self-transformation. The story encourages us to look deep within ourselves and find the courage to allow our soul to dance again.*"
Marcela Grant, author of *Luminous Mountain*

For Mom, Dad, Neil, Nancy, Daniel, Lauren, Leigh, Fab, Kaitlyn and Victoria, who never forgot about what I'd hidden away.

For my dear sister-friends, Ann-Michelle, Elizabeth, Joanna and Marnie, who were right beside me as I opened the door.

For my wise angel teachers, Eimear, Harriett, Jacqueline and Rita, who helped me pull out the really big weeds.

For poet and peacemaker, Mattie J.T. Stepanek, who tinkled the first bells.

And most of all, for my beloveds: Chris, Liam, Declan and Pumpkin, who always saw that I could dance, cheered me on when I first started to play my music and continue to scatter new seeds with me in our garden. I will always love you.

Foreword
by Harriett Simon Salinger

The Flowering House may be the next step on your personal path. I subscribe to the "Yellow Brick Road" philosophy: that each of us is on a very unique journey, where our greatest invitation is to pay attention and to notice what draws us. What is calling you? What attracts your attention? These are the questions that this simple, charming story poses.

I so firmly hold in my heart that there is a unique kernel in each of us; I believe that it is this uniqueness that we are all longing to go home to. And how we travel to get there is an unknown journey.

After 30 years as a psychotherapist and then making my own transformative journey to working in personal development where I've coached hundreds of people over the past 17 years, I know that there is no one truth, one way, or even one set of steps I can offer to someone who is asking, "How do I find my authentic path?" There are as many paths as people. I may be able to suggest that you go and take a peek over there, or try smelling that flower, and then we can talk about what you've noticed.

What I can offer those who are beginning to get a whiff of something else beckoning them are some inquiries or contexts that may be helpful:

- You need that first whiff: it is important to recognize that something smells good out there, without making yourself feel bad for smelling it or allowing it to invalidate the truth of where you are now.
- The yellow brick in the road that catches your attention is not the same as anyone else's: you will not follow the same path as your mother, sister, husband, neighbour or best friend.
- Be open to the role that creativity may play on your path; broaden your definition of creativity beyond the arts and music to embrace that how you live your life is also a work of art and your personal unfolding is in fact a creative act.
- You may fear whiffing something that lies outside what you have known is possible. Fear is going to be present if you are committed to your authentic path; it is important to shift the expectation from "No Fear" to "Know Fear"; get to know how fear shows up for you, and then you can work with it.
- The alternative to walking your yellow brick road is walking the generic, predictable, status quo road; on this road, you do not free your spirit or liberate your soul.
- Liberation requires that we find a deep well of courage and mix it with curiosity and self-questioning.
- When you challenge your status quo, life will rise to meet you; with each step of liberation, you allow more light in you and more light on the planet.

Ultimately, a context and intention that has supported me on my path has been "Trust Life." In that, we're able to hold that everything—loss, sadness, anger and all the emotions, truly all of our experiences along the way—is a part of this magnificent journey called life. There is nothing wrong or bad in the evolution of each person. And we can see that what we may have viewed as mistakes or bad steps in our own lives were actually the next magnificent lessons in our unfolding.

This is true for Camilla in *The Flowering House*, as it has been true for Paige in her journey. Having coached Paige for several years as she began to follow the whiffs of "something more" in her life, I am so proud and honoured these years later to be included in this expression of her story.

I see *The Flowering House* as a reflection of her deep compassion and desire to share with other women who are awakening to their own unique journeys. I bless Paige and I bless the lives of all those who are drawn to and touched by this story.

Harriett

Wise Woman Coaching

www.hssalinger.com

Camilla had a very tidy house. At least that's what everybody thought. Camilla knew better.

No one would have ever guessed her secret. Camilla's front yard was immaculate. She had a neat kitchen and a beautiful living room. But there were closets and rooms in Camilla's house that she hadn't been in for years. She kept the doors to these rooms shut tight so she didn't have to think about, or look at, the mess that lay hidden behind them.

And that wasn't even the worst of it...

Camilla kept the door that led to her backyard tightly locked up, except when she had to throw something out. Over the years, she had discarded junky furniture, bags of old clothing, used paint cans and broken toys, and these items were scattered in piles throughout the backyard. Amidst all this garbage, the only thing that could grow was weeds. Some of the weeds in Camilla's backyard were bigger than Camilla herself. She was glad she had a high fence.

Sometimes, Camilla was disappointed that she wasn't able to enjoy her backyard. She wondered what she was missing, especially when her friends talked about having barbeques or just spending quiet time in a lounge chair. But it made Camilla too tired to even think about where to begin cleaning.

Besides, Camilla was too busy keeping the front yard beautiful. She painted the door and the windowsills whenever they looked dirty. She planted pretty flowers in straight rows along her front pathway. She even trimmed the lawn so that every piece of grass was the same height. After all, she reasoned, neighbours passed the front of her house every day on their way to work or school. She didn't want them to think she was messy.

Camilla also spent a great deal of time keeping the living room presentable, because it was where she planned to serve tea and cookies to her friends. She wanted it to be perfect! Unfortunately, Camilla never seemed to get around to inviting guests over.

Every few weeks, she changed her mind about what colour looked best in the room. She would put a new coat of paint on the walls, make new curtains and buy new rugs. This week, Camilla's living room was blue, and she was already wondering if it was a bit too dark.

Camilla had been changing the living room decor and trimming each blade of grass in the front yard for so long that she couldn't remember the last time she'd seen her friends. When they passed by her house, they thought about stopping to talk with her, but she always looked too busy, so they would continue walking past.

One night, when Camilla was getting into bed, she felt something uncomfortable in her chest. At first, she thought maybe she'd pulled a muscle while she was hanging a new painting in the living room. Then she felt it again and realized that it wasn't an injury; there seemed to be a little twinge in her heart.

For a brief moment, Camilla wondered if it might be sadness she was feeling, but that thought was scary, and she immediately chased it away. "Don't be silly, Camilla," she told herself. "You can't possibly be unhappy. You have the most beautiful front yard in town." And the new yellow colour she had just chosen for the living room was sure to be cheery.

To assure herself that everything was just fine, Camilla got out of bed to do one more thing. As she walked down the hallway, she heard a faint sound from behind the door to one of the bedrooms that she'd kept closed up for years. Ignoring it, Camilla continued down the stairs. She went out to the front yard with some scissors and cut a few flowers from her garden. She put them in a clear glass vase and placed the vase on the table in the living room. There—now everything was perfect!

Perfect—except that, when Camilla awoke the next morning, she still felt an ache in her heart. She quickly decided that she must need some company and immediately phoned her friends, Ted and Beatrice, to invite them over for tea. When they accepted, Camilla suddenly realized how much she needed to do to get ready.

She worked so fast that she looked like a tornado going through the house. She planted some new red flowers in the front gardens and repainted the front door to match them. She evened off a few stray pieces of grass. In the living room, she dusted, vacuumed, polished and fluffed. Satisfied that everything was ready for her friends' visit, Camilla finished off by baking a dozen cookies.

Ted and Beatrice showed up right on time, with looks of amazement as they entered Camilla's house. "Why, Camilla, your home is beautiful!" said Ted.

"I've never seen anything like this," said Beatrice, thinking of her somewhat messy, but comfy, den.

"Fantastic!" echoed Ted, as he quickly removed his sneakers, taking note of the sparkling clean floor.

Beatrice made sure to walk carefully through the living room. She didn't want to accidentally knock any of the lovely vases or brush against any of the paintings. "Please, sit down," Camilla urged. "I'm just going to bring out our tea." Ted and Beatrice sat delicately at the edge of the couch.

"So, Camilla," started Ted, "it's been a long time since we've seen you. What have you been up to?"

"Well," replied Camilla, as she poured the tea into her finest china cups, "I've been very busy indeed. There's always so much to be done around here. The front yard requires a lot of care."

"Oh, yes, I can imagine," offered Ted. "Your flowers are gorgeous."

Camilla smiled, glad that he had noticed, although she also felt a bit disappointed that neither of her friends had said anything about her perfectly pedicured lawn.

"These dishes are lovely," commented Beatrice, holding her teacup as gently as she could manage.

"Thank you," replied Camilla. Then there was an awkward silence. To break it, Camilla asked, "So, what have the two of you been doing lately?"

Ted became animated, almost leaping from his seat from excitement, until he remembered that he might upset the cushions. "I've been taking jazz dancing classes at the community centre," Ted explained. "My instructor suggested I dance at the town talent show this year."

"That's nice," responded Camilla softly, remembering how she used to dance when she was younger.

"I've been going once a week to help at the retirement home," Beatrice said. "Sometimes we do crafts together, or read or just chat. I've made a lot of new friends."

"That's terrific," replied Camilla, forcing a smile. She was suddenly aware of a pressure in her chest again. Emotion constricted her throat, and Camilla felt tears welling up, but she quickly pushed them down.

"Well, I think we'd better go now," Ted said. "We're meeting some friends to go bowling tonight."

Seeing the look on Camilla's face, Beatrice quickly offered, "Would you like to come with us?"

"Oh, no," said Camilla, smiling again. "I'm much too busy tonight. I need to get things cleaned up."

Ted and Beatrice thanked Camilla for the tea and cookies, put on their shoes and left.

Camilla immediately began to clean up the dishes and wipe the table. "Well, there," she assured herself, "now I can't be sad. I just had a nice visit with two good friends. And they did say that my house was beautiful."

When Camilla was brushing her teeth that evening, however, she realized that her heart was aching even more than it had before her friends had come over. This awareness made Camilla feel very unsettled, and she was unsure where to turn.

"What could possibly be wrong with me?" she wondered. Almost at the same moment this question arose, Camilla heard the little sound again, coming from down the hallway. It seemed a bit louder than the night before. She tiptoed toward the room and pressed her ear up against the closed door.

Every few seconds, there was a bit of muted music, like tiny bells jingling on the tips of elves' slippers. Camilla was curious. What could it be behind this closed door making such an inviting sound? At the same time, Camilla was frightened of opening the door, knowing that she hadn't looked in there in years. She didn't even remember what was hidden in the room—certainly nothing she needed. Or so she thought.

Slowly, cautiously, Camilla inched the door open. Moonlight shone through the window and illuminated an old wooden chest. On the top of it, something moved slightly, and the bells gave out another tinkle. Camilla walked slowly toward the sound, still not certain of its source. "Oh my goodness," she exclaimed as she got closer. "It's my old music box."

Camilla bent over to take a closer look. As the music box came into focus, memories flooded in and tears welled up in her eyes. Suddenly, it felt to Camilla as though she were back in the childhood bedroom she had shared with her older sister, Julia. She recalled how she would wind the music box with the little key, and how the tiny dancer perched on top would begin to spin. After Julia tucked Camilla into her bed, Camilla would dream of being a ballerina.

Wiping tears from her face, Camilla picked up the music box and turned to leave the room. "This needs to be dusted off," she bravely decided. As she pulled the door shut behind her, she paused to take one more look back at the closed wooden trunk.

After cleaning the music box, Camilla wound it up and placed it on her bedside table. It played a light, gentle melody, and as she fell off to sleep, Camilla dreamt that she was beginning to dance.

The next morning, Camilla awoke feeling different somehow. Instead of rushing into the many chores that she usually tackled, she enjoyed her breakfast slowly, savouring the taste of the food. As she ate, she wondered about what else she'd left in that closed room upstairs. She was especially curious about what might be hidden in that chest.

Gathering her broom and dustpan, a large pail of water and some rags, Camilla prepared to enter the room. She took a deep breath and opened the door. She took a step back. Boy, did it smell musty! She hadn't realized, in the glow of the previous night, how bad it really was. She was tempted to turn around and leave, but something compelled Camilla to stay and do the much-needed work.

Let's get that window open and let in some fresh air, she thought. With a cool breeze coming in, Camilla set to her task. She washed the windows and swept the floor. She scrubbed the walls. She unpacked some of the boxes that lay around the room. Finally, Camilla walked slowly toward the old chest. She wiped the dust off the top so that it was completely clean. Gently, she unlatched the hinge and lifted the lid.

The first thing Camilla spotted was her old art set. Opening up the case, she was amazed by the variety of colours of paints and crayons inside. There were several paintbrushes and a set of pastels. "I'd forgotten all about this!" she mused. Camilla liked using different colours to create beauty; her living room was proof of that!

Then she discovered some paintings that she'd done when she was younger. She took each one out, admiring them as she laid them out on the floor beside her. As she dug a little deeper into the chest, Camilla came upon an old photo album. She flipped through the pages, giggling at pictures of herself learning to ride a bike and playing dress-up with Julia.

Then Camilla turned another page and felt her heart skip a beat when she saw a picture of herself with a cast on her leg. She recalled vividly the dance recital when she had just missed that turn and come down on the stage with her leg twisted awkwardly beneath her. The pain of that time flooded back—not of the injury, but of the embarrassment she'd felt, and the loneliness she'd endured during the months that followed, when she was unable to dance with her friends. Today, all these years later, Camilla finally allowed herself to cry.

The next day, Camilla realized that her heart didn't hurt as much. She moved through her house with new eyes and a lighter step. She decided to replace some of the fancy, store-bought paintings in her living room with some of her own creations that she'd found in the chest upstairs. It didn't matter to

Camilla that they might not be perfect. She especially loved the painting she had done of her family's flower garden, and she placed it above her couch. It had so many colourful flowers that it would match her living room no matter what.

Today, however, Camilla wasn't thinking about changing the colour of her living room. She was much more interested in digging deeper in the chest.

Camilla's mornings seemed to fly by so quickly when she was sorting through things in the previously closed up bedroom. She found music that she used to love and spent time listening to it. Then she discovered, hidden at the back of the closet, something lacy and pink. She pulled out her old ballerina tutu and also found the matching slippers. Tentatively, Camilla put them on.

In the privacy of the room, and with her music playing, Camilla began to dance. It didn't matter that no one was watching her—in fact, it made it easier for her to move whichever way she felt like moving. At first, she was not very graceful and almost fell over when she tried to spin.

Camilla had often wondered why she hadn't returned to dancing after her broken leg, and now she understood a bit better. It was not easy to be a beginner again after winning all those dance competitions when she was younger. And yet, in the freedom and joy of these movements, something began to come alive deep within Camilla that made all the missteps worthwhile.

Passing by her house, Ted and Beatrice heard something they hadn't heard before: music mixed with the glorious sound of Camilla's laughter. "I wonder what's going on in there," said Ted. Beatrice was equally perplexed and suggested they knock on the door and find out.

Camilla glided down the staircase and greeted her friends, sweaty and smiling.

"Wow, Camilla, look at you!" Beatrice exclaimed. "Have you been dancing?"

"Yes, actually," responded Camilla. "I've found some old things and have been trying them on for fun."

"Well, we won't keep you from it," said Ted. "Perhaps you'd consider joining me in the talent show next month."

As they walked down the front walkway, Beatrice turned back. "You look beautiful, Camilla!"

As she waved goodbye, Camilla thought, *yes, and I am happy, too.*

As the grass grew more uneven in her front yard, Camilla found herself unlocking more and more rooms and closets and clearing space in her home. Eventually, Camilla came to the door that led out to the backyard. Looking out the window, Camilla pictured herself in a wonderful garden, sitting in a comfortable lounge chair, listening to music and feeling the warmth of the sunshine on her face. She took off the lock that had kept this door shut, and threw it in the garbage.

All week, Camilla worked hard, clearing away the old furniture and throwing out broken toys and garbage.

The weeds that had grown larger than Camilla were a little more difficult to get rid of. After all, they had been putting down roots for years. Camilla tried and tried to pull them out, but she just couldn't get a good enough grip on them. She was upset that she wasn't strong enough to do this, and felt disappointed that just this one thing stood in the way of completing her beautiful backyard.

That evening, Camilla was listening to music and thinking about the challenge of the weeds. Maybe she just didn't have the right tools. Maybe she just needed some help. She was reluctant to call her friends. She knew that they would gladly help her, but she also realized that, to enlist their help, she would have to allow them to see how wild and messy her backyard had become.

The next day, Camilla glanced out at the backyard again. She was so close. Swallowing her pride, and with a catch in her throat, Camilla picked up the phone.

Soon, Ted arrived with a spade and Beatrice with a ladder. With a little help from her friends, Camilla succeeded in pulling out all the weeds in the yard. Ted even mowed the lawn, and the three of them celebrated their efforts with a nice pitcher of lemonade.

With the backyard cleared, there was more open space than Camilla had ever imagined. "Are you going to plant some of the pretty yellow and red flowers like the ones in the front yard?" asked Beatrice.

"No," replied Camilla, "I've got something entirely different in mind." She reached into her pocket and pulled out a package of wildflower seeds. Camilla let the seeds scatter randomly as she danced joyfully around the yard.

Heartsong

I have a song, deep in my heart,
And only I can hear it.
If I close my eyes and sit very still
It is so easy to listen to my song.
When my eyes are open and
I am so busy and moving and busy,
If I take time and listen very hard,
I can still hear my Heartsong.
It makes me feel happy.
Happier than ever.
Happier than everywhere
And everything and everyone
In the whole wide world.
Happy like thinking about
Going to Heaven when I die.
My Heartsong sounds like this - -
> *I love you! I love you!*
> *How happy you can be!*
> *How happy you can make*
> *This whole world be!*

And sometimes it's other
Tunes and words, too,
But it always sings the
Same special feeling to me.
It makes me think of
Jamie, and Katie and Stevie,
And other wonderful things.
This is *my* special song.
But do you know what?
Everyone has a special song
Inside their hearts!
Everyone in the whole wide world
Has their own special heart-song.
If you believe in magical, musical hearts,
And if you believe you *can* be happy,
Then you, too, will hear *your* song.

"Heartsongs" by Mattie J.T. Stepanek (March, 1996)
Used with permission from Journey Through Heartsongs
by Mattie J.T. Stepanek (Hyperion, 2002)
For more information: www.mattieonline.com

Awakening to Your Heart's Desire

Camilla's story is my story. And I suspect it is the story of many of us, especially women, who make the journey from hidden truths, keeping up appearances and disconnection from self, to feeling restless, listening to the whispers, courageously opening scary doors, and in time moving closer and closer to authenticity and true joy.

Twelve years ago, I had hidden away the best parts of myself. I was in an unhappy, repressive marriage and hiding that fact from everyone else in my life. In our home, all of my treasured belongings were hidden away in one room that was for me, as he did not like any of my art, photos or furniture. I was in a deep, dark cave and didn't know how to find my way out—my inner light began to fade.

My life became one of appearances. I left a job I enjoyed for one that offered more prestige, a bigger title and more money, and ended up feeling trapped and unhappy in that as well. From the outside, it must have seemed as though I had it all, but those closest to me knew I was losing what I loved most about myself.

Thankfully, one of the "ringing bells" in my life was hiring a life coach—a career I had just begun training for. My dear Harriett almost frightened me away with her matter-of-fact proclamation that I was at heart a "healer," but the shivers and goosebumps revealed that my body knew a truth of which I was not yet aware.

One of my first homework assignments was to make a list of my tolerations—those things that were draining energy from my life. When I topped 100 items, I looked at the list in desperation and wondered how I would ever begin to turn my life around. But I would—because now I was awake and couldn't turn back.

I started to spend time listening to the whispers and heeding their call. I journaled, did *The Artist's Way* and went on long walks. Eventually, I let go of things that were not serving me, including my marriage and secure job. I courageously opened doors I had closed off, and I sought help to uproot the really big weeds.

In less than two years, I relocated to a home that I filled with my treasured items, trained to be a life coach and launched my own business, became a student of reiki, and met the love of my life. (We have now been happily married for almost ten years and have two lovely boys together.)

I am so appreciative of the life I have created. And I am grateful for the challenging time I had to go through in order to arrive here. I now experience profound joy on a daily basis, I love many and feel loved by many, and I am able to use my gifts in service to others. I am also aware that new dreams are always being born, and I look forward to that evolution. Most of all, I am deeply grateful to all those whose lives have touched mine and who have assisted me along my path. Namaste.

—Paige

How to Use this Journal

We all know that the journey is never truly finished, as there is always more to discover about ourselves, more to open up to, more to let in, more to move toward. I invite you to use the guided journal process that follows as an inquiry and reflective practice. Suggested exercises are an invitation to put new awareness into action.

The path to discovering and living our true heart's desires is not a linear one. It is a many-layered spiral, leading us forward, and then deeper, winding us round in what feels like a random series of events, until we are able to look back on our lives and see the patterns and synchronicities.

Therefore, this journal is meant to be explored in whatever way appeals most to you: from beginning to end if you want to follow Camilla's path; by choosing titles that attract you most if you want to follow your heart; or by simply opening to a page and jumping around intuitively.

Another powerful use of the journal is to form a group of women and use the questions in this book as a guide to your discussions. A circle of supportive, like-minded women creates support and accountability, which are good companions on this journey.

Most of all, enjoy yourself. There is no end point, no perfect conclusion to reach; as long as we are still alive (and we are eternal beings), we never really get it done.

A joy-full, authentic, creative life awaits you. The world is waiting for the full expression of your unique gifts. Journey well.

"There came a time when the risk to remain tight in the bud was more painful than the risk it took to blossom."—Anais Nin

"If there is one door in the castle you have been told not to go through, you must. Otherwise you'll just be rearranging furniture in rooms you've already been in."—Anne Lamott

1. Living the Lie: Hiding from the Truth

Camilla had a very tidy house. At least that's what everybody thought. Camilla knew better.

No one would have ever guessed her secret. Camilla's front yard was immaculate. She had a neat kitchen and a beautiful living room. But there were closets and rooms in Camilla's house that she hadn't been in for years. She kept the doors to these rooms shut tight so she didn't have to think about, or look at, the mess that lay hidden behind them.

And that wasn't even the worst of it...

Camilla kept the door that led to her backyard tightly locked up, except when she had to throw something out. Over the years, she had discarded junky furniture, bags of old clothing, used paint cans and broken toys, and these items were scattered in piles throughout the backyard. Amidst all this garbage, the only thing that could grow was weeds. Some of the weeds in Camilla's backyard were bigger than Camilla herself. She was glad she had a high fence.

Where is your life secretly messy?

What do you do to hide the weeds that are growing bigger than you?

Suggestion: Make a list (could be five items or 100 items) of things that you are "tolerating." A toleration can be as simple as an unsewn button or an email you need to respond to, or as complex as a job that is draining your energy or a house you need to renovate. Don't worry at this point about how to deal with the tolerations—this activity is simply to bring them into your awareness.

"All truths are easy to understand once they are discovered; the point is to discover them." —Galileo Galilei

2. Feeling Trapped: Overwhelmed by Current Circumstances

Sometimes, Camilla was disappointed that she wasn't able to enjoy her backyard. She wondered what she was missing, especially when her friends talked about having barbeques or just spending quiet time in a lounge chair. But it made Camilla too tired to even think about where to begin cleaning.

"Do the difficult things while they are easy and do the great things while they are small. A journey of a thousand miles must begin with a single step." —Lao Tzu

What is one big task that has you feeling overwhelmed?
How could you break it into smaller steps that would allow you to begin?

What present circumstance makes you too tired to even think about? If you can identify that this is what you *do not* want, you can also identify its opposite, what you *do* want. What is it that you *do* want?

Suggestion: Write again what you *do* want, in vivid detail, as though it has already been fulfilled. How is your life different, now that this has happened? Breathe that in; imagine it fully and feel what it feels like in this new version of your life. Spend two minutes at the beginning and end of each day, fully imagining this fulfilled desire.

"When you acknowledge what you do not want, and then ask yourself, "What is it that I do want?" you begin a gradual shift into the telling of your new story and into a much-improved point of attraction." —Abraham, excerpted from the book, *Money and the Law of Attraction: Learning to Attract Health, Wealth & Happiness,* by Jerry and Esther Hicks

Resource: *Ask and It Is Given,* by Jerry and Esther Hicks, www.abraham-hicks.com

3. Keeping Busy: Maintaining Distractions

Besides, Camilla was too busy keeping the front yard beautiful. She painted the door and the windowsills whenever they looked dirty. She planted pretty flowers in straight rows along her front pathway. She even trimmed the lawn so that every piece of grass was the same height.

"It is an ironic habit of human beings to run faster when they have lost their way." —Rollo May

What distractions or "busy projects" do you turn to that keep you from facing what really needs your attention?

How do your distractions serve you?

What do your distractions keep you from? What might you discover if the distractions were eliminated?

What opportunity for joy have you been "putting aside"?

Suggestion: Eliminate your most common distractions (TV, Internet browsing, snacking, etc.) for one week. Allow yourself to be with the void and to feel the feelings that rise up. Ask yourself, "What would I most like to do right now?" Then do it—go for that walk, take out that paintbrush, phone that old friend. Feel how it feels to follow a natural impulse.

"People don't want their lives fixed. Nobody wants their problems solved. Their dramas. Their distractions. Their stories resolved. Their messes cleaned up. Because what would they have left? Just the big scary unknown."
—Chuck Palahniuk

4. Looking Good for Others: Striving for Perfection

After all, she reasoned, neighbours passed the front of her house every day on their way to work or school. She didn't want them to think she was messy.

Camilla also spent a great deal of time keeping the living room presentable, because it was where she planned to serve tea and cookies to her friends. She wanted it to be perfect!

Every few weeks, she changed her mind about what colour looked best in the room. She would put a new coat of paint on the walls, make new curtains and buy new rugs. This week, Camilla's living room was blue, and she was already wondering if it was a bit too dark.

Are there things you keep changing in your life?
What are you never quite satisfied with?

Whose approval are you seeking?

Can you identify the voices in your head that push you to achieve perfection? Develop a short personal mantra as an antidote to these voices. (You'll know it's right for you when it creates a deep breath.)

What might you be missing out on because of your desire for perfection?

How would your life change if you were gentler with yourself?

Suggestion: Develop a relationship with the perfectionist within you. Draw/paint her, interview her, find out what her higher purpose is for you, and make friends with her.

"Perfectionism is not a quest for the best. It is a pursuit of the worst in ourselves, the part that tells us that nothing we do will ever be good enough—that we should try again."—Julia Cameron

Resource: *The Gifts of Imperfection,* by Brené Brown

5. Physical Cues: The Beginning of Pain

One night, when Camilla was getting into bed, she felt something uncomfortable in her chest. At first, she thought that maybe she'd pulled a muscle while she was hanging a new painting in the living room. Then she felt it again and realized that it wasn't an injury; there seemed to be a little twinge in her heart.

"Neurobiologist Dr. Candace Pert had proven … [that] our emotions reside physically in our bodies and interact with our cells and tissues."
—From *Anatomy of the Spirit*, Caroline Myss

Often, when we are out of touch with our authentic dreams and true desires, we are living our lives primarily from the head. Reaching for balance, we get signals from our hearts, either in the form of emotions, restlessness or physical cues.

Where in your body do you routinely feel uncomfortable?

What do you think your body is saying to you?

In the still, quiet moments, what message does your heart have for you?

Suggestion: Find a quiet place to sit or lie down where you won't be disturbed. Take time to focus on your breath—each inhalation and exhalation. Take at least 10 deep, soothing breaths. Now imagine a stream of energy flowing up from the core of Mother Earth through the soles of your feet, up your legs, through your core, and encircling your heart. Next, imagine a stream of light flowing down from the heavens through the crown of your head, down your neck and throat, soothing your shoulders, and encircling your heart. Rest in your attention to your heart area, and allow it to be fully nurtured by the combined energies that are swirling around it. Imagine breathing in and out from your heart.

"It is only with the heart that one can see rightly; what is essential is invisible to the eye."—Antoine de Saint-Exupéry

Resource: *Anatomy of the Spirit*, Caroline Myss

6. Ignoring the First Whisper

For a brief moment, Camilla wondered if it might be sadness she was feeling, but that thought was scary, and she immediately chased it away. "Don't be silly, Camilla," she told herself. "You can't possibly be unhappy. You have the most beautiful front yard in town." And the new yellow colour she had just chosen for the living room was sure to be cheery.

To assure herself that everything was just fine, Camilla got out of bed to do one more thing. As she walked down the hallway, she heard a faint sound from behind the door to one of the bedrooms that she'd kept closed up for years. Ignoring it, Camilla continued down the stairs. She went out to the front yard with some scissors and cut a few flowers from her garden. She put them in a clear glass vase and placed the vase on the table in the living room. There—now everything was perfect!

"Sometimes all it takes is a whisper"—Anonymous

The first hints of our heart's desires often come as faint whispers. Many of us ignore the first twinge of knowing that we are not living our passions fully or dismiss it as something else. We want desperately to reassure ourselves that our current life is just fine, that change is not necessary.

How do the faint whispers show up in your life (e.g., you sense an inner prompting, a friend mentions something, a book comes into your life, you hear a particular song)?

What fears arise when you think of changing your life to more fully live your dreams?

Suggestion: Become more aware of your own intuitions and the subtle signs from the universe. Keep a small journal of recurring thoughts, the lyrics of the song you keep hearing, and the symbolism of an animal that keeps crossing your path. Believe that all experiences coming into your life have meaning. What are the messages in these whispers?

"God speaks in the silence of the heart. Listening is the beginning of prayer." —Mother Teresa

Resource: *Animal Speak,* by Ted Andrews

7. External Praise Versus Internal Fulfillment

"Oh, yes, I can imagine," offered Ted. "Your flowers are gorgeous."

Camilla smiled, glad that he had noticed, although she also felt a bit disappointed that neither of her friends had said anything about her perfectly pedicured lawn.

"These dishes are lovely," commented Beatrice, holding her teacup as gently as she could manage.

"Thank you," replied Camilla.

"A man desires praise that he may be reassured, that he may be quit of his doubting of himself; he is indifferent to applause when he is confident of success."—Alec Waugh

The praise we seek from others can never fill the gaps that exist in our own opinions of ourselves. While we may seek external acknowledgement for our accomplishments, it usually falls short of assuring us of our own value and worth. This important work is an "inside job."

In what ways are your decisions and actions motivated by wanting to please others and gain their approval or recognition?

What would you need to do, or who would you like to be, in order to improve your own opinion of yourself?

What if you could accept yourself fully, just as you are right now? How would that change your relationship with yourself?

Suggestion: For the next week, keep a journal and write down each time you do or say something with the goal of winning someone's approval, praise or admiration. At the same time, write out three affirmations about yourself (starting with "I am…"). These could be things you like about yourself, things you often hear others say about you, or qualities you hope to grow into more. Repeat these affirmations daily, out loud if possible.

Resources: Anything by Louise L. Hay; *The Six Pillars of Self Esteem*, by Nathaniel Brandon

8. Letting Envy Be Your Teacher

"I've been taking jazz dancing classes at the community centre," Ted explained. "My instructor suggested I dance at the town talent show this year."

"That's nice," responded Camilla softly, remembering how she used to dance when she was younger.

"I've been going once a week to help at the retirement home," Beatrice said. "Sometimes we do crafts together, or read or just chat. I've made a lot of new friends."

"That's terrific," replied Camilla, forcing a smile. She was suddenly aware of a pressure in her chest again. Emotion constricted her throat, and Camilla felt tears welling up, but she quickly pushed them down.

When others share with us how they are living their heart's desires, we often get pangs of envy. We have a choice in that moment: to feel bitter ("It figures that she gets to … She's always been lucky!") or to realize that envy is a teacher that shows us where we are unfulfilled in our own lives, and begin the task of meeting our own needs.

Of whom do you feel envious? Of what in particular are you envious?

How are you denying the presence of this quality, experience or material object in your own life?

What do you envision this thing providing for you that you do not currently experience?

Suggestion: Let envy be your teacher. When you find yourself feeling critical of others for their choices or actions, ask yourself if this resentment points to something you are missing in your life experience. If so, decide on one small action step toward its realization. If you are feeling courageous, have a conversation with the person you envy: let the person know that you admire him or her, that you are looking to create more _____ in your life as well, and ask for the person's input on how to get there.

"Envy can be a positive motivator. Let it inspire you to work harder for what you want."—Robert Bringle

9. Owning the Discomfort: The Signs Get Louder

When Camilla was brushing her teeth that evening, however, she realized that her heart was aching even more than it had before her friends had come over. This awareness made Camilla feel very unsettled, and she was unsure where to turn.

"What could possibly be wrong with me?" she wondered. Almost at the same moment this question arose, Camilla heard the little sound again, coming from down the hallway. It seemed a bit louder than the night before. She tiptoed toward the room and pressed her ear up against the closed door.

"The first step … shall be to lose the way."—Galway Kinnell

When we ignore the first whispers of our heart's longing, typically our discomfort grows. Messages get louder until we are ready to be truthful with ourselves about what we are feeling. Only when we acknowledge the restlessness, emptiness or confusion do we allow hints of the answers to appear.

What uncomfortable emotions have you been denying?

What might be the benefit of allowing yourself to be "lost"?

How does self-doubt show up for you and how much authority do you give it?

What signs are beginning to show up in your life that invite you to open previously closed doors?

Suggestion: When you become aware of an uncomfortable emotion, take the time to fully be with the discomfort. Sit with your sadness or disappointment or confusion without trying to chase it away, change it or resolve it. Just be. Breathe. It is only through our acceptance of the truth of where we are in this moment that we make room for the journey toward greater joy, fulfillment or clarity.

"Have patience with everything unresolved in your heart and try to love the questions themselves as if they were locked rooms or books written in a very foreign language. Don't search for the answers, which could not be given to you now, because you would not be able to live them. And the point is to live everything. Live the questions now. Perhaps then, someday far in the future, you will gradually, without even noticing it, live your way into the answer." —Rainer Maria Rilke

Resource: *Callings*, by Gregg Levoy

10.   Opening the Door: First Courageous Act

Every few seconds, there was a bit of muted music, like tiny bells jingling on the tips of elves' slippers. Camilla was curious. What could it be behind this closed door making such an inviting sound? At the same time, Camilla was frightened of opening the door, knowing that she hadn't looked in there in years. She didn't even remember what was hidden in the room—certainly nothing she needed. Or so she thought.

Slowly, cautiously, Camilla inched the door open. Moonlight shone through the window and illuminated an old wooden chest. On the top of it, something moved slightly, and the bells gave out another tinkle. Camilla walked slowly toward the sound, still not certain of its source. "Oh my goodness," she exclaimed as she got closer. "It's my old music box."

Wiping tears from her face, Camilla picked up the music box and turned to leave the room. "This needs to be dusted off," she bravely decided.

"Life shrinks or expands in proportion to one's courage."—Anais Nin

What "hidden room" in your life makes you feel both curious and frightened?

What's currently "tinkling" in your background?

What one item, interest, ability or relationship in your life "needs to be dusted off"?

Suggestion: Listening for the whispers, and paying attention to the small signs in life, can lead you intuitively to places your conscious mind would not consider. The next time you get a "whisper" in your life, when your heart beats a little faster, act courageously and follow its lead. Sign up for the workshop, make the phone call, read the book. See where it takes you…

"It may be when we no longer know what to do,
We have come to our real work,
And that when we no longer know which way to go,
We have begun our real journey."
—Wendell Berry

Resource: *The Artist's Way,* by Julia Cameron

11. Paying Attention to Dreams and Intuitions

After cleaning the music box, Camilla wound it up and placed it on her bedside table. It played a light, gentle melody, and as she fell off to sleep, Camilla dreamt that she was beginning to dance.

"Those who dream by day are cognizant of many things which escape those who dream only by night."— Douglas Adams

We all have access to a universal wisdom that flows through us as individuals in the form of intuition, dreams and synchronicities. We can either allow this flow, or pinch it off. It is always available to us, though we must learn to let it in by believing it is possible. It is helpful to begin to pay attention to the ways intuition works best for us—some of us just "know," some feel (get a gut reaction), some "hear" guidance and others can visualize. Acknowledge when an intuition or dream does provide you with guidance, and try to find someone with whom to share your intuition development.

When do you most allow yourself to be guided by your intuition?

How could you more fully develop and trust your intuitions?

Who is the person you most trust to listen to your deepest dreams and the intuitions you are having about your heart's desire?

How could you further cultivate this relationship?

Suggestion: Right before you go to bed, use a Gratitude Journal to record five things you are grateful for. Then hold something in your mind that you would like to attract into your life experience. Picture it fully and allow yourself to feel the feelings of this scenario as though it were already present in your life.

"Stay calm. Be brave. Wait for the signs."—Thomas King

"The only real valuable thing is intuition."—Albert Einstein

Resources: *Creative Visualization,* by Shakti Gawain; *Practical Intuition,* by Laura Day; *Sark's Journal and Play!book,* by Sark

12. Feeling and Acting Differently

The next morning, Camilla awoke feeling different somehow. Instead of rushing into the many chores that she usually tackled, she enjoyed her breakfast slowly, savouring the taste of the food. She wondered about what else she had left in that closed room upstairs. She was especially curious about what might be hidden in that chest.

"Every day of our lives we are on the verge of making those slight changes that would make all the difference."—Mignon McLaughlin

"Stopping is a spiritual practice." —Dr. Robert Holden

What happens in your life when you intentionally relax and slow down?

What routine in your daily life could you alter or slow down?

How can you find more balance between the "doing" and "being" sides of your life?

What are you curious about—in your own life and in the world around you?

Suggestion: Change the way you start your day. Rise 15 minutes earlier (if need be) so that you can do something mindful that appeals to you: gentle stretching, yoga, prayer, meditation, journaling. Do this for at least two weeks and note whether it changes the way you feel and how you flow through the rest of your day. Begin to practise the art of being more fully present.

"If we take care of the moments, the years will take care of themselves." —Maria Edgeworth

Resource: *The Power of Now,* by Eckhart Tolle

13. Being Tempted to Turn Away

Gathering her broom and dustpan, a large pail of water and some rags, Camilla prepared to enter the room. She took a deep breath and opened the door. She took a step back. Boy, did it smell musty! She hadn't realized, in the glow of the previous night, how bad it really was. She was tempted to turn around and leave, but something compelled Camilla to stay and do the much-needed work.

It is exciting to have the breakthrough, the insight that seems to show us how to live our heart's desire. After the shine of the initial discovery has worn off, however, it is easy to be overwhelmed when we realize how much hard work lies before us. It is the fork in the road—do we plow ahead despite the obstacles, or do we retreat to our simpler and safer, yet unfulfilling, life?

What is your typical pattern when you face obstacles?

In the past, what has happened when you've shrunk back from a challenge? What has happened when you've plowed ahead, despite fear?

How have you overcome fears in your life?

How do you know the difference between real fear and perceived fear?

What do you want your relationship with fear to be?

Suggestion: Try this guided visualization: Get yourself in a relaxed position. Take at least 10 deep breaths until you are completely relaxed. Imagine that you are walking through a beautiful forest. Hear the birds singing, and feel a gentle breeze on your face. The path is clear and you feel joyful as you walk. As you look ahead, you see a stone wall. As you get closer, you see that it is more than 12 feet high, and runs as far as you can see in both directions. What do you do?

"At the worst, a house unkempt cannot be so distressing as a life unlived." —Rose Macaulay

14. Discovering What Has Been Hinted at All Along

The first thing Camilla spotted was her old art set. Opening up the case, she was amazed by the variety of colours of paints and crayons inside. There were several paintbrushes, and a set of pastels. "I'd forgotten all about this!" she mused. Camilla liked using different colours to create beauty; her living room was proof of that!

"Until we see what we are, we cannot take steps to become what we should be." —Charlotte Perkins Gilman

Sometimes, it takes looking back before we can move forward. Often the interests we held when we were younger provide valuable information about what our hearts may be longing for. It is not unusual to discover that there have been glimpses of our most authentic expressions throughout our lives, unacknowledged amidst the responsibilities and demands of daily life.

What did you most enjoy doing/playing when you were a child?
Why did you like those activities?

Find a trunk or box or photo album from your younger life that you could pull out and look through. What does it reveal?

When you look at pictures from your early life (three to six years old) how would you describe your essence?

What are the parts of yourself that were more fully expressed when you were younger?

What are the ways that those parts of you find expression now, even if in a slightly different format?

How could you cultivate more of the things that bring you joy and fulfillment in your life today?

Suggestion: Choose one of your childhood activities from the above list, and make a plan to do it this week. Paint, bake, swing, play in a sandbox—do this simply for the joy of it, and release any inhibitions you have.

"Put your ear down close to your soul and listen hard." —Anne Sexton

Resource: *I Could Do Anything (If I Only Knew What It Was),* by Barbara Sher

15. Facing and Releasing Pain

Then Camilla turned another page and felt her heart skip a beat when she saw a picture of herself with a cast on her leg. She recalled vividly the dance recital when she had just missed that turn and come down on the stage with her leg twisted awkwardly beneath her. The pain of that time flooded back—not of the injury, but of the embarrassment she'd felt and the loneliness she'd endured during the months that followed, when she was unable to dance with her friends. Today, all these years later, Camilla finally allowed herself to cry.

"If you haven't had at least a slight poetic crack in the heart, you have been cheated by nature."—Phyllis Battelle

It is painful to uncover an unfulfilled heart's desire. It is easier to be unconscious of our deeper longings, or to dismiss them as fanciful ideas from our youth, than to truly look at a dream that has not yet manifested and acknowledge some of the accompanying emotions—sorrow, regret, disappointment. Some of us have never reached for a dream because of self-imposed limitations and not wanting to fail; others of us have tried to achieve a dream, faced a true obstacle and never dared to dream a new dream.

What longings or dreams from the past have you not allowed yourself to hold onto?

Have you allowed yourself to update the vision and reclaim it? What would it take for you to do that?

If you are not able to identify any dream from your younger days, become aware of your self-talk when you think of having a big dream now. If you hear any version of "How silly; who are you to…?", you've likely had the beginnings of many dreams in the past, but they were squelched by your own self-imposed limitations. Shifting this self-talk is key to allowing true desires to arise.

Suggestion: In a journal, make two columns. On the left-hand side, write with your dominant hand, "I would like to…" and fill in the blank all the way down the column. On the right-hand side, write with your non-dominant hand, "How I feel about that." Simply observe where you are judging or limiting yourself.

"Your pain is the breaking of the shell that encloses your understanding."—Khalil Gibran

16. Honouring Your Own Creative Work

The next day, Camilla realized that her heart didn't hurt as much. She moved through her house with new eyes and a lighter step. She decided to replace some of the fancy, store-bought paintings in her living room with some of her own creations that she'd found in the chest upstairs. It didn't matter to Camilla that they might not be perfect. She especially loved the painting she had done of her family's flower garden, and she placed it above her couch. It had so many colourful flowers that that it would match her living room no matter what.

"The way you treat yourself sets the standard for others."—Sonya Friedman

"The important thing is to feel your music, really feel it and believe it."—Ray Charles

Before others can honour and appreciate your creative gifts, you first must honour and appreciate them yourself.

What does creativity mean to you?

If you're afraid (or are sure) that you aren't creative, how could you expand your definition of what being "creative" means?

What creative pursuits bring you the most joy?

How do you make space and time for yourself to be creative?

When you have created something (e.g., a wonderful meal, a craft, a song, a blog post), what do you or could you do to honour and appreciate that creation?

Suggestion: When you've completed the next inspired creation, take time to appreciate yourself and the creative act before sharing it with others. Whether you take a moment to say to yourself "Gorgeous—good job!" or take five minutes to savour the taste of the cake you baked, appreciating yourself first is integral to cultivating a creative life and ensuring that you are not relying solely upon the opinions of others.

"If the only prayer you ever say in your entire life is 'Thank You,' it will be enough." —Meister Eckhardt

17. Time Flies

Camilla's mornings seemed to fly by so quickly when she was sorting through things in the previously closed up bedroom. She found music that she used to love and spent time listening to it. Then she discovered, hidden at the back of the closet, something lacy and pink. She pulled out her old ballerina tutu and also found the matching slippers. Tentatively, Camilla put them on.

"Time flies when you're having fun." —Anonymous

Leading researcher Mihaly Csikszentmihalyi proposes that people are most joyful when they are in a state of *flow*. Flow is achieved when one is in a state of complete concentration or absorption in a given activity. Many skilled athletes, musicians and artists will refer to the flow state as being "in the zone" or "in the groove."

Recall a time when you were completely absorbed in an activity and felt a sense of fulfillment, engagement and alignment—as though your skills were being fully utilized. What were you doing?

What happens when you are in a state of flow?

Suggestion: It has been noted that mindfulness, yoga, meditation, the Alexander Technique and martial arts all aid in the increased capacity for flow states as they train and improve attention. Choose one of these activities and commit to a regular weekly or daily practice for a period of three or more months. Note how this practice affects your attention, stress levels and sense of well-being.

"Let yourself be silently drawn by the stronger pull of what you really love." —Rumi

Resources: *Flow: The Psychology of Optimal Experience,* by Mihaly Csikszentmihalyi; *Wherever You Go, There You Are: Mindfulness Meditation in Everyday Life,* by Jon Kabat-Zinn

18. Being Willing to Be a Beginner

In the privacy of the room, and with her music playing, Camilla began to dance. It didn't matter that no one was watching her—in fact, it made it easier for her to move in whichever way she felt like moving. At first, she was not very graceful and almost fell over when she tried to spin.

Camilla had often wondered why she hadn't returned to dancing after her broken leg, and now she understood a bit better. It was not easy to be a beginner again after winning all those dance competitions when she was younger. And yet, in the freedom and joy of these movements, something began to come alive deep within Camilla that made all the missteps worthwhile.

"To live a creative life, we must lose our fear of being wrong."—Joseph Chilton Pearce

It takes courage to allow oneself to be a beginner—to give oneself full permission to not know, to ask for help, to make mistakes, to stumble. We must begin to recognize and appreciate the gifts the beginner brings: new curiosity, a heightened attentiveness, an inquiring attitude and a fresh perspective. When one dares to take off the mask and reveal a creative idea or speak a personal truth, one risks vulnerability for joy, authenticity and connection.

Recall a time you were a beginner—a new school or job, the first time trying a new sport, driving a car, travelling to a foreign country. What mix of emotions did you experience?

How did you move through your initial fears?

What is something you've been putting off or hesitating to start for fear of being a beginner?

What would you do if you knew you couldn't fail?

Suggestion: Choose one activity/interest/creative pursuit that you've always wanted to try but just have never "signed up" for. Research what you would need to do to begin (e.g., take a course, buy materials/equipment, put aside money to travel, etc.) and set a realistic goal for beginning.

"The real voyage of discovery consists not of seeking new lands, but in seeing with new eyes."—Proust

19.   People Noticing Changes in You

Camilla glided down the staircase and greeted her friends, sweaty and smiling.

"Wow, Camilla, look at you!" Beatrice exclaimed. "Have you been dancing?"

"Yes, actually," responded Camilla. "I've found some old things and have been trying them on for fun."

"Well, we won't keep you from it," said Ted. "Perhaps you'd consider joining me in the talent show next month."

As they walked down the front walkway, Beatrice turned back. "You look beautiful, Camilla!"

As she waved goodbye, Camilla thought, yes, and I am happy, too.

"Friends are the mirror reflecting the truth of who we are."—Anonymous

"Clean your finger before you point at my spots." —Benjamin Franklin

As you begin to step more fully into expressing and sharing your creative gifts, you will begin to get feedback from those around you. Some friends and family, especially those who are living their creative dreams, will see and be able to reflect to you your joy, beauty and fulfillment. Others will feel threatened by the path you are now on. They may attempt to "put you back into your place," simply because they are more comfortable with the "old" you.

How will you balance the feedback you receive from others about the changes they see in you with your own feelings and sense of transformation?

How can you prepare yourself to respond to those who are not supportive of the dreams you are pursuing?

Suggestion: Identify one or two close friends or family members who seem to be fulfilled in their own pursuits. Once you are on your way to exploring your heart's desires, take the risk to share with these friends and ask them for input or feedback.

"Be who you are and say what you feel because those who mind don't matter and those who matter don't mind."—Dr. Seuss

20. Envisioning the Dream Fulfilled

As the grass grew more uneven in her front yard, Camilla found herself unlocking more and more rooms and closets and clearing space in her home. Eventually, Camilla came to the door that led out to the backyard. Looking out the window, Camilla pictured herself in a wonderful garden, sitting in the comfortable lounge chair, listening to music and feeling the warmth of the sunshine on her face. She took off the lock that had kept this door shut, and threw it in the garbage.

All week, Camilla worked hard, clearing away the old furniture and throwing out broken toys and garbage.

"Faith sees a beautiful blossom in a bulb, a lovely garden in a seed, and a giant oak in an acorn."—William Arthur Ward

As you take steps into the pursuits that bring you joy, you will begin to experience new-found energy. When you are able to form a vision of living the life you've always wanted, the overwhelming task of getting there from where you currently stand starts to unfold. Synchronicities happen, new people show up in your life, and it becomes clear what you must do. Now is the time to do it. Clear away the old and let go of what no longer serves you. Hold firm to your vision of the future.

How can you build in more time for daydreaming?

Where can you "play with your future vision" best? Soaking in the bathtub, driving in the car, journaling, walking in nature?

What is one step you could take now to clear out the old or welcome in the new?

Who can you share your vision with; who will hold you lovingly accountable?

Suggestion: Create a dream board. Begin by ripping out images from magazines or printing images you are drawn to. Focus on images that would support you living the life of your dreams or achieving a specific feeling. Play with the images to collage them onto a board. (Bristol board is fine.) Pictures are more powerful than words.

"Until one is committed, there is hesitancy, the chance to draw back, always ineffectiveness ... the moment one definitely commits oneself, then providence moves too. All sorts of things occur to help one that would not otherwise have occurred ... Whatever you can do or dream you can, begin it. Boldness has genius, power and magic in it. Begin it now!"—Goethe

Resource: www.dreambigcollection.com, by Jack Canfield

21. Asking for Help: Being Vulnerable

The weeds that had grown larger than Camilla were a little more difficult to get rid of. After all, they had been putting down roots for years. Camilla tried and tried to pull them out, but she just couldn't get a good enough grip on them. She was upset that she wasn't strong enough to do this, and felt disappointed that just this one thing stood in the way of completing her beautiful backyard.

That evening, Camilla was listening to music and thinking about the challenge of the weeds. Maybe she just didn't have the right tools. Maybe she just needed some help. She was reluctant to call her friends. She knew that they would gladly help her, but she also realized that, to get their help, she would have to allow them to see how wild and messy her backyard had become.

The next day, Camilla glanced out at the backyard again. She was so close. Swallowing her pride, and with a catch in her throat, Camilla picked up the phone.

"Vulnerabiity is our most accurate measurement of courage."—Brené Brown

As you begin to live aspects of your desired life, and you let go of things that no longer serve you, it is not uncommon to be stopped in your tracks by an obstacle that you are not able to clear on your own. It is easy to become derailed at this point, just short of attracting your desire. Most of us have "really big weeds" that require tools we don't have on hand, and need help to uproot. This is the point when you must risk being vulnerable and ask for help.

What "big weeds" are you currently facing in your life?

What help do you require to clear them?

What gets in the way of you asking for help?

Suggestion: Begin practising the art of asking for help. Identify one small (or big) thing that someone could do for you that would make your life easier or richer. Ask that person to help you with this.

"Something we were withholding made us weak, until we found out it was ourselves."—Robert Frost

Resource: *Mayday! Asking for Help in Times of Need,* by M. Nora Klaver

22. Clearing Space for the New

With a little help from her friends, Camilla succeeded in pulling out all the weeds in the yard. With the backyard cleared, there was more open space than Camilla had ever imagined.

"Grace fills empty spaces, but it can only enter where there is a void to receive it."—Simone Weil

Spirit works best with a vacuum. When your life (calendar, home, heart and mind) is filled to the brim with what already is, there is no room for what could be. When you let go of the commitments, events, items, relationships, work and dramas that are no longer serving you, you may find yourself with more time and space than you thought possible. And then you may feel very uncomfortable. Sit with your discomfort; treasure the silence; keep an open heart. You'll be amazed by what begins to appear in your life.

What old things (e.g., items, patterns, relationships) are no longer serving you and are you ready to let go of in order to create space for the new?

When in your life have you "been in the void"? What did you learn about yourself during those times?

What does your historical wisdom remind you about that would be helpful to remember now?

Suggestion: Identify three things that no longer serve you. Let go of one of those things.

"Do you have the patience to wait 'till your mud settles and the water is clear? Can you remain unmoving 'till the right action arises by itself?"—Lao Tzu

Resource: *Clearing the Clutter for Good Feng Shui,* by Mary Lambert

23. Sowing New Seeds: Living Your Heart's Desire

"Are you going to plant some of the pretty yellow and red flowers like the ones in the front yard?" asked Beatrice.

"No," replied Camilla, "I've got something entirely different in mind." She reached into her pocket and pulled out a package of wildflower seeds. Camilla let the seeds scatter randomly as she danced joyfully around the yard.

"Tell me, what is it you plan to do with your one wild and precious life?" —Mary Oliver

"The beauty of life is that it takes turns that are sometimes bigger than your wildest dreams."—Freida Pinto

It is important to recognize when the changes we have dreamed of are happening, to celebrate how we are making new choices, attracting new circumstances and living more authentically.

Take time now to record some of the internal and external transformations that you see taking place in your life.

What are you grateful for?

Suggestion: If you feel inspired to do so, share your list with a dear and trusted friend. Ask him or her to share anything the person sees that is shifting/changing for you.

"Let me light my lamp," says the star, "and never debate if it will help to dispel the darkness."—Rabindranath Tagore

Resources: *Be Happy; Happiness Now!; Authentic Success*; and *Shift Happens,* by Dr. Robert Holden

24. Sharing Your Gifts

"Her work, I really think her work
is finding what her real work is
and doing it,
her work, her own work,
her being human,
her being in the world."
—Ursula K. Le Guin

All of us are searching—for who we really are, for inspiration, for connection, for a sense of purpose, for a calling. Your calling may not be as much about what you do during the day as it is about who you are being as you move through that day.

We are awakening to the spiritual side of human life and longing to live it in our everyday lives. The danger is in getting lost in the search, continually seeking and never finding peace and fulfillment in the present. We must remind each other that it is not in the end destination that we find joy; the process of living our truth is joyful. And once we fulfill a dream, new dreams are born.

We must now turn our attention to the present and accept that we are perfect in this very moment. We need nothing more—not more education, a bigger house, or a spiritual breakthrough—in order to fulfill our purpose, our destiny. We need only to be willing to know ourselves, to be ourselves and then to share who we are with others.

At your essence, what are the qualities you most value in yourself?

What would your "life well lived" look like? If you wrote the story of your life now, what would be the key themes?

How could you more fully share your authentic gifts with others?

"There is a prayer that lives in the center of your heart. If you pray it, it will change your life. How does it begin?" —Dr. Matthew Anderson

About the Author

Paige Stirling Fox is a life coach and facilitator of numerous personal growth and spiritual programs and workshops. She believes in the power of circles of women and has created and led many programs, including Women Circling the Earth, a year-long retreat and coaching program; and Breathing Space, circles for women who have survived cancer.

Paige earned an honours degree in psychology and a certificate in adult education, and she has completed coach training with Coach U. She is a Reiki master and a certified labyrinth facilitator.

Paige currently works as an early literacy specialist and lives with her husband and two children in Ontario, Canada.

Contact Paige directly at Paige@thefloweringhouse.com

Website: www.thefloweringhouse.com

www.facebook.com/PaigeStirlingFox

Twitter:@FloweringHouse

CPSIA information can be obtained
at www.ICGtesting.com
Printed in the USA
LVIW020117020512
279935LV00002B